Danse Macabre

and

Havanaise

For Violin and Orchestra
in Full Score

Camille Saint-Saëns

DOVER PUBLICATIONS, INC.
Mineola, New York

£9.95

Bibliographical Note

This Dover edition, first published in 2005, is an unabridged republication in one volume of two works originally published by A. Durand & Fils, Paris: *Danse Macabre – Poème Symphonique,* 1875 and *Havanaise,* 1888.

International Standard Book Number: 0-486-44147-4

Manufactured in the United States of America
Dover Publications, Inc., 31 East 2nd Street, Mineola, N.Y. 11501

Contents

Dance Macabre   1

Havanaise   55

Instrumentation

1 Piccolo – Petite Flûte
2 Flutes – Grande Flûtes
2 Oboes – Hautbois
2 Bb Clarinets – Clarinettes en Sib
2 Bassoons – Bassons

1st and 2nd Horns in G – Cors en Sol
3rd and 4th Horns in D – Cors en Ré
2 Trumpets in D – Trompettes en Ré
1st and 2nd Trombones – Trombones
3rd Trombone and Tuba – Trombone et Tuba

Xylophone – Xilophone
3 Timpani in D, A, and G – Timbales en Ré La Sol
Triangle – Triangle
Cymbal – Cymbales
Bass Drum – Grosse Caise

Harp – Harpe

Solo Violin – 1 Violon Solo
Tuned to G-D-A-Eb

1st Violins – Violons
2nd Violins – Violons
Violas – Altos
Cellos – Violoncelles
String Basses – Contrebasses

DANSE MACABRE

POÈME SYMPHONIQUE

C. SAINT-SAËNS
Op. 40

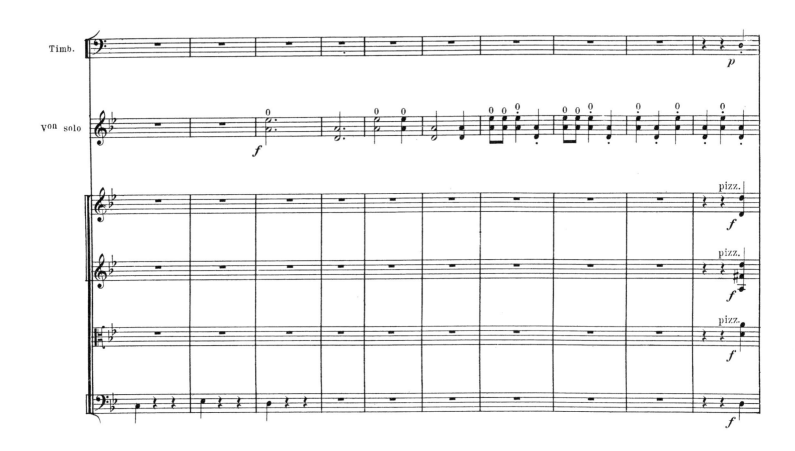

4

12

14

19

F

30

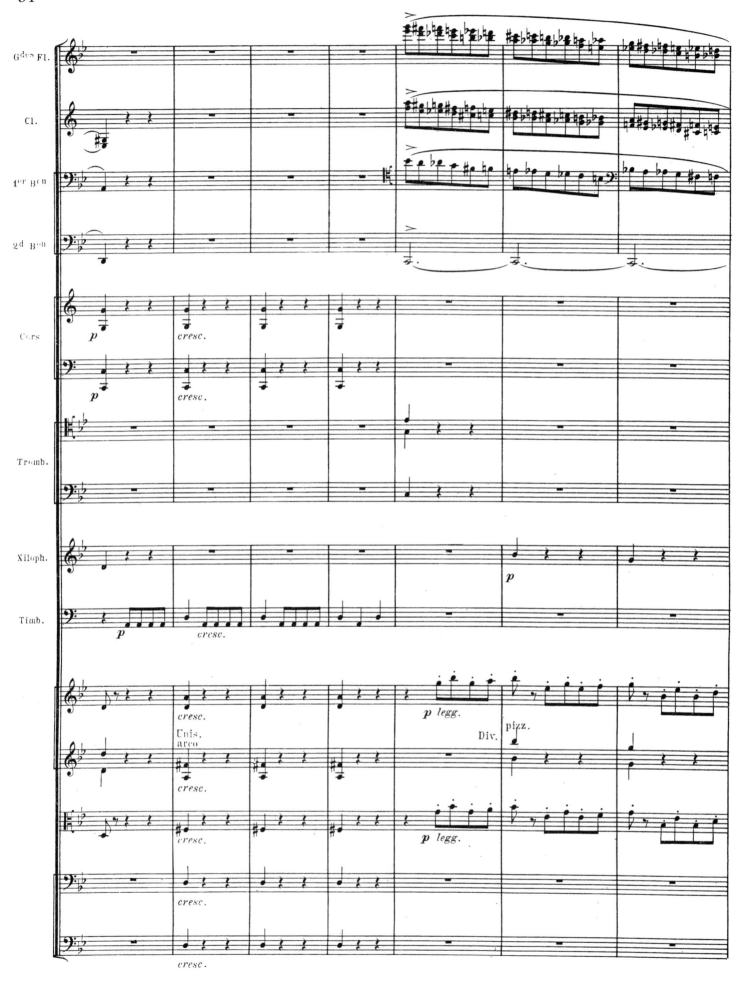

44

46

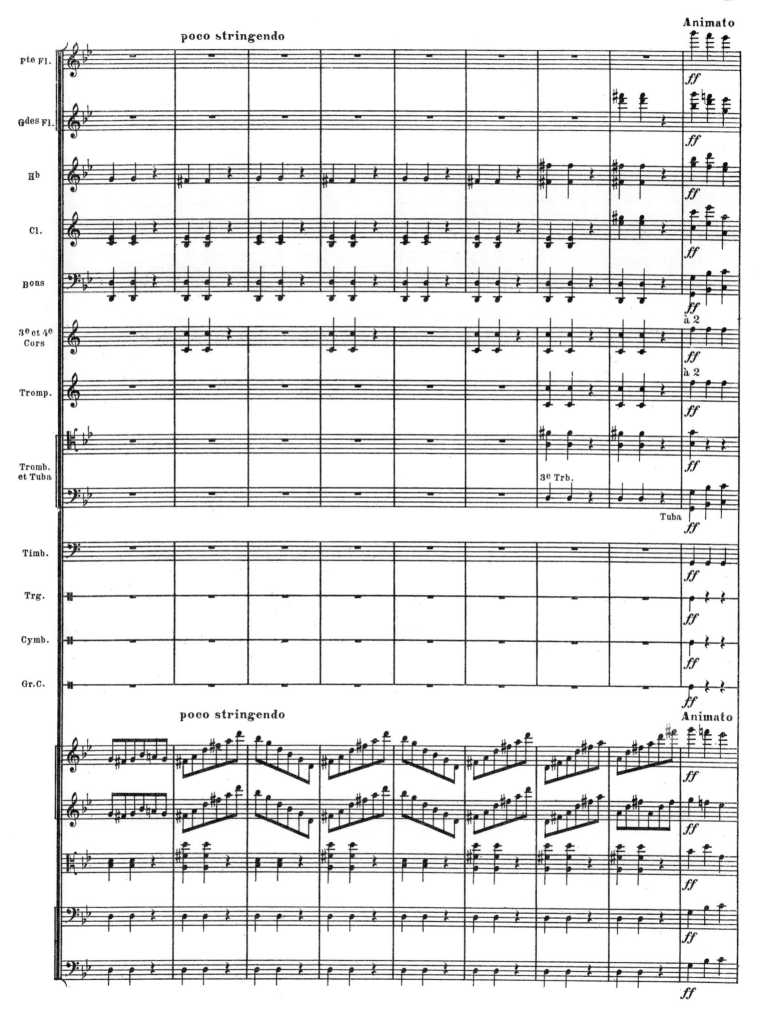

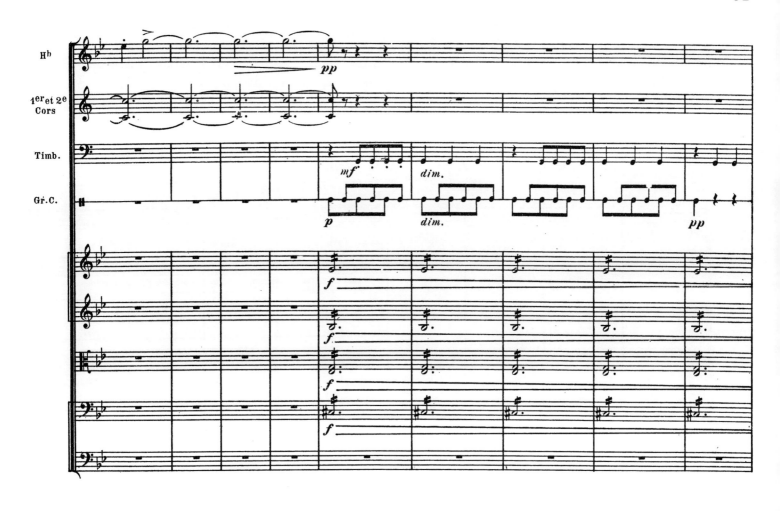

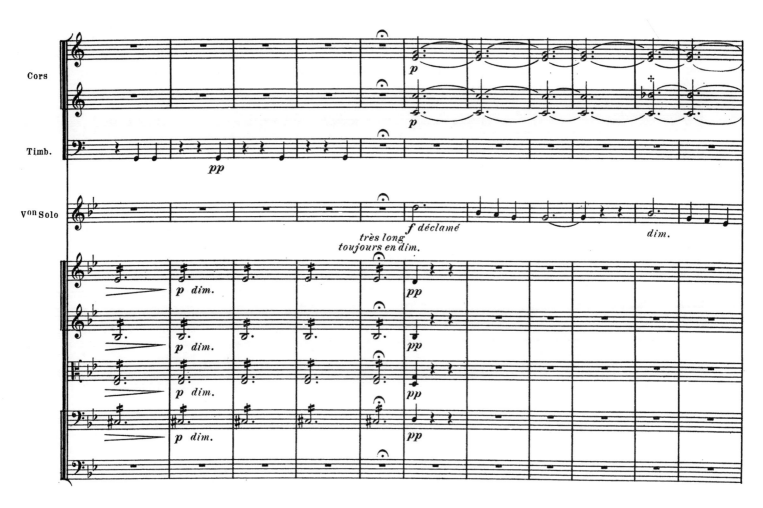

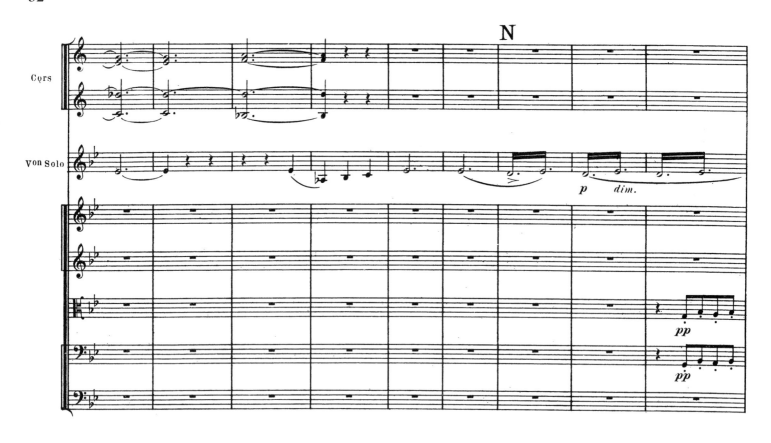

Havanaise

Instrumentation

2 Flutes –Flûtes
2 Oboes – Hautbois
2 Clarinets in A – Clarinettes en La
2 Bassoons – Bassons

1 Horn in E – Cor en Mi

1 Horn in D – Cor en Ré
2 Trumpets in E – Trompettes en Mi

Timpani in B and E – Timbales Si - Mi

Solo Violin – Violon Solo

Violins (1st and 2nd) – Violons
Violas – Altos
Cellos – Violoncelles
String Basses – Contrebasses

HAVANAISE

Op: 83

CAMILLE SAINT-SAËNS
(1835-1921)

Cor en MI

Timb.

Cor en MI

sempre pizz.

Allegretto